PAUL DAVIS

Chord Academy

A Beginner's Guide to Mastering the Keyboard

ISBN: 9798848537789
IMPRINT: Independently published

Visit the Chord Academy YouTube Channel:

https://tinyurl.com/ChordAcademy

Table of contents

Welcome to Chord Academy!

This book will teach you how to play chords (a group of notes that make up a harmony) and how to read chordal music using helpful tips and fun methods so you can start playing music quickly.

You will also learn music theory, which **defines the elements that form harmony, melody, and rhythm**. We will help you understand the core concepts of how music works in a very simple way. You will learn fun songs, simple rhythms, and how to combine different types of chords along our musical journey.

Our goal is to start playing music right away. Let's get started!

Hand and Finger Numbers

Hand placement on the piano: We play the piano using our left hand on the lower keys on the keyboard and our right hand on the middle to high keys on the keyboard.

We number our fingers as a guide to make it easy to play the notes on the piano.

When we play, we make sure our hands are curved and relaxed.

LH means Left Hand.
RH means Right Hand.

Fingers are numbered as follows:

Thumbs are 1
Pointing fingers are 2
Middle fingers are 3
Ring fingers are 4
Pinky fingers are 5

Practice speaking each finger out loud.

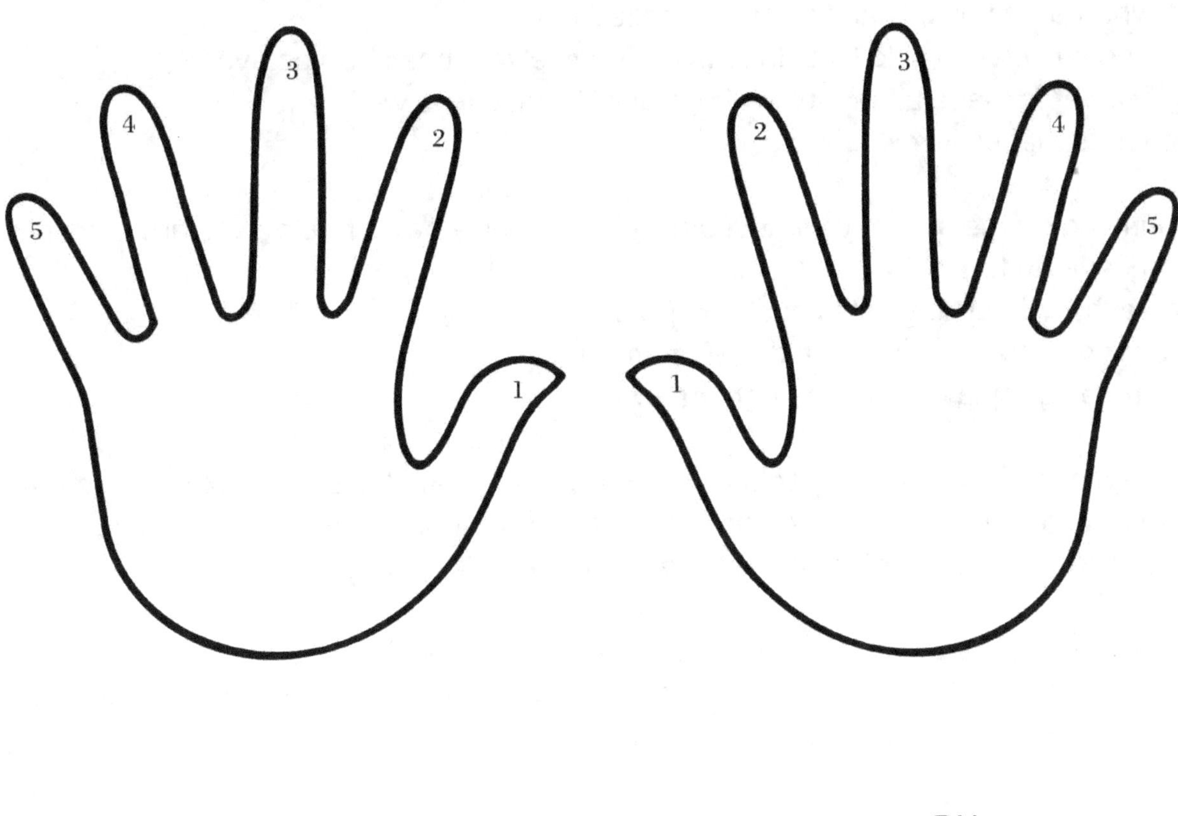

Piano Basics

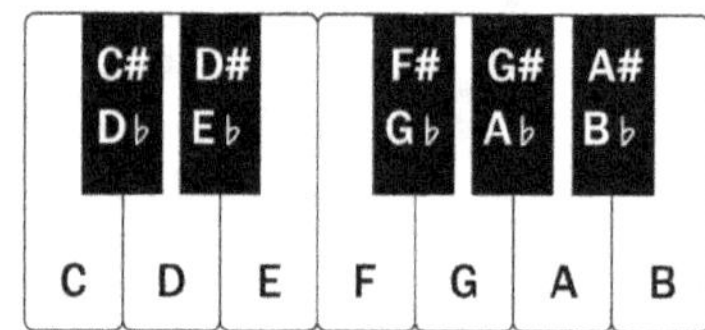 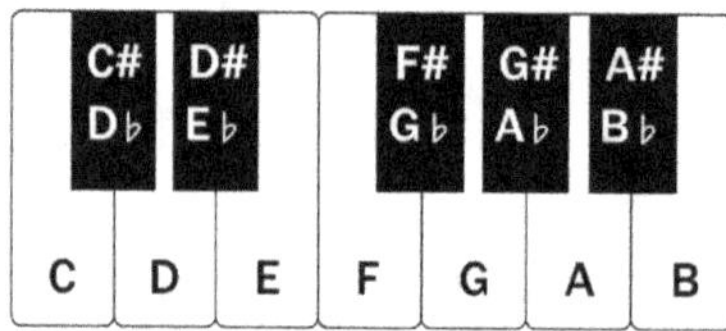 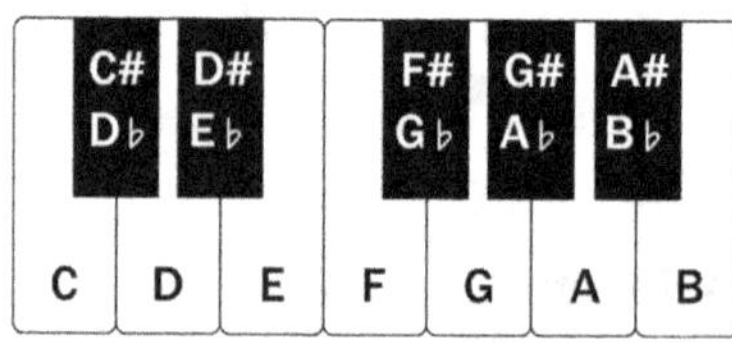

Octave 1 low tones   Octave 2 mid tones   Octave 3 higher tones

A Keyboard has black and white keys called notes.
Each note is placed side by side to make up twelve tones of an octave.
An "octave" is made up of 7 black keys and 5 white keys with 12 *tones*.
Each note makes its own tone.

Depending on the size of your keyboard you may only have 1 octave, a larger keyboard could have up to 8 octaves.
The keyboard has low notes and high notes.
The low notes are played with the left hand.
High notes are played with the right hand.

The keyboard has 12 notes per octave. There are 7 white keys and 5 black keys that make up those twelve notes. All black keys have two names. The name that we use for the key depends on whether we are playing up the piano or down.

For example, if we are playing the black key between the white C and D keys going up the piano, the black key would be called C Sharp. When we move down the keyboard or to the left, we would call the same key D Flat.

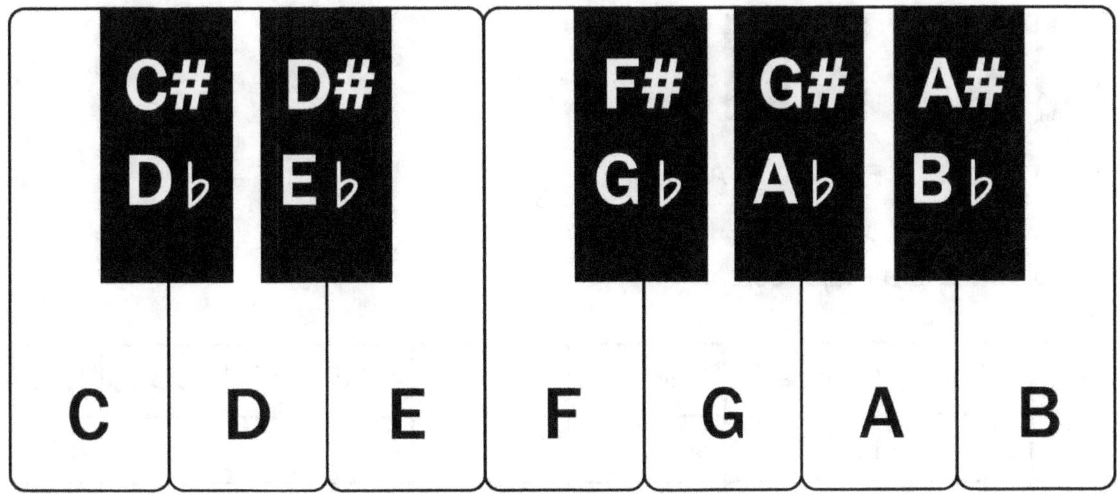

Melody, Chords, and the Song

Song

There are two types of Songs:
1. Vocal - A vocal song is a combination of words, chords and melodies.
2. Instrumental - An instrumental song is a combination of chords and melodies without words.

Melody

A vocal melody is sung and an instrumental melody is played to create a memorable experience. This is accomplished by using tones or words.

Major Scales

There are 12 keys per octave and each one of these keys has a major scale associated with it.

A major scale is made up of eight notes, three whole steps followed by a half step, then three more whole steps, followed by a half step.

A whole step skips the note next to it. Half steps do not skip any notes.

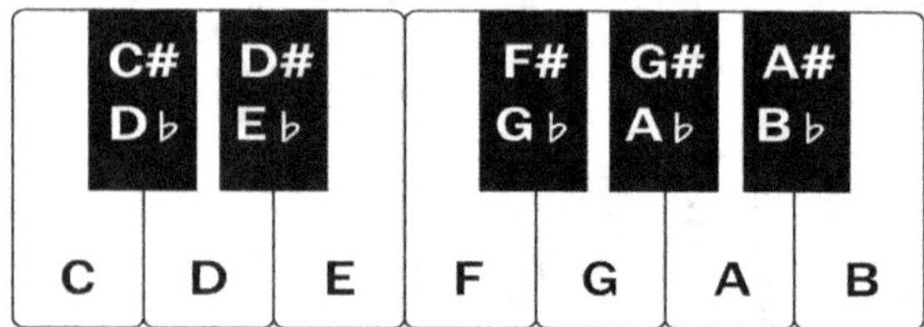

For example, this is a major scale:

Whole	Whole	Whole	Half	Whole	Whole	Whole	Half
1	2	3	4	5	6	7	8
C	D	E	F	G	A	B	C

Another example, Eb has a Major Scale associated with it. Below is the Major Scale for Eb:

Whole	Whole	Whole	Half	Whole	Whole	Whole	Half
1	2	3	4	5	6	7	8
Eb	F	G	Ab	Bb	C	D	E

Major Chords

A major chord is used to form the harmony of a melody.
In the "Piano Chords Chart" example each chord can be Major, Minor, Dominant or seventh.

A *slash* chord (G/B) simply indicates Right-hand/Left-hand, played **"over the top of"** … where the second letter is the name of the *single note* you'll play with your LEFT hand and the first letter is the name of the *chord* you will play with your RIGHT hand, simultaneously.

How to identify major chords

The distance between two notes is called an interval.
A chord is a combination of two (commonly three) or more notes played simultaneously.

Generally, there are five kinds of basic chords which make up the basis of what most other chords are built upon:

- Major chord is the 1st, 3rd, and 5th note in the Major scale
- Minor chord is the 1st, 3rd, and 5th note in the Minor scale (a Minor scale is the same as a Major scale, except some of the notes included in the scale are flat notes).
- Dominant or seventh is the 1st, 3rd, 5th and flat 7th in the Major scale
- Major seventh is the 1st, 3rd, 5th and 7th note in the Major scale
- Minor seventh is the 1st, flat 3rd, 5th, flat 6th, and 7th note in the Minor scale

Piano Chords Chart

	Major	Minor	seventh	Minor seventh	Major seventh
C	C	Cm	C7	Cm7	CM7
D	D	Dm	D7	Dm7	DM7
E	E	Em	E7	Em7	EM7
F	F	Fm	F7	Fm7	FM7
G	G	Gm	G7	Gm7	GM7
A	A	Am	A7	Am7	AM7
B	B	Bm	B7	Bm7	BM7

Exercise 1: Play all 7 major chords (C,D,E,F,G,A,B) in the Major column on the "Piano Chords" chart in succession.

We refer to the black keys as "up" and the white keys as "down"

Hint.   C are all *down* keys
D is 3rd key up
E is 3rd key up
F is all *down* keys
G is all *down* keys
A is 3rd key up
B is 3rd and 5th key up

Exercise 2:   Using the first row on the "Piano Chords" chart below, play the "C" row for each chord (C Major, C Minor, C Seventh, C Minor Seventh, C Major Seventh) in succession.

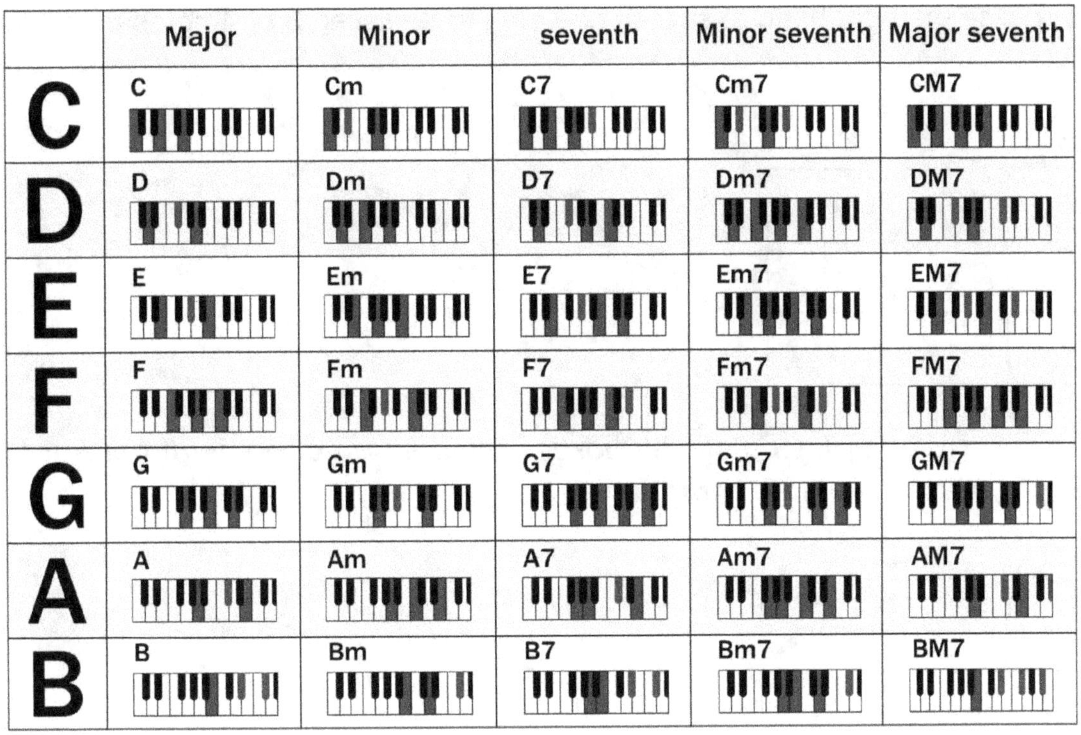

	Major	Minor	seventh	Minor seventh	Major seventh
C	C	Cm	C7	Cm7	CM7
D	D	Dm	D7	Dm7	DM7
E	E	Em	E7	Em7	EM7
F	F	Fm	F7	Fm7	FM7
G	G	Gm	G7	Gm7	GM7
A	A	Am	A7	Am7	AM7
B	B	Bm	B7	Bm7	BM7

<u>5 Quick Tips to Start Playing Songs</u>

1. Familiarize yourself with the songs by listening to them before you start playing each song in the song book.

2. Remember to use the right hand using the 1, 3 and 5 fingers when playing chords.

3. When using both hands, use the left hand to play the singular left hand note of the chord. Use the right hand to stretch and play the existing 3 or 4 notes in the right hand.

C chord

1 finger	1-3- 5 fingers
C	C E G
LH	RH

Reminder: When playing slash chords play the first chord with the right hand and play the single note with the left hand.

Slash Chords C/D

1 finger	1- 3- 5 fingers
D	C E G
LH	RH

4. When playing four finger chords use the 1, 2, 3, 4 or 5 fingers.

Example:

1	2	3	4	fingers
C	E	G	B	CMajor 7

5. Take on the challenge of playing the songs with the concepts you have learned

<u>**Resources**</u>

Visit the YouTube website for more tips and examples of how to play the song book tips and new music at:

https://tinyurl.com/ChordAcademy

Biggest selection of popular chords on piano:

https://www.ultimate-guitar.com/

Guide to all chords in the piano world:

https://www.pianochord.org/

Song Book

Happy Birthday To You	Twinkle Twinkle Little Star
Mary Had A Little Lamb	Take Me Out To The Ball Game
London Bridge	A-Tisket A-Tasket
Are You Sleeping	When The Saints Go Marching
Hot Cross Buns	Greensleeves
America The Beautiful	Amazing Grace
Star Spangled Banner	It Had To Be You

Happy Birthday To You ¾ TIME

```
      G             D
Happy birthday to you,
      D7            G
Happy birthday to you,
      G7                  D   C
Happy birthday, dear David,
      G         D   G
Happy birthday to you.


   G                D
May God bless you dear,
   D7               G
May God bless you dear,
   G7                      D  C
May God bless you dear Susan,
      G             D   G
Happy birthday to you.


   G                D
How  old are  you,
   D7               G
How  old are  you,
   G7                     D    C
How  old are  you, David,
      G         D7 G
Happy birthday to you.
```

<u>**Mary Had a Little Lamb 4/4 Time**</u>

```
C              Dm            G          C
Mary had a little lamb, little lamb, little lamb

 C                   F        G              C
Mary had a little lamb whose fleece was white as snow.

   C                           Dm         G        C
And everywhere that Mary went, Mary went, Mary went,

   C                      F        G        C
everywhere that Mary went the lamb was sure to go.

   C                   Dm              G              C
It followed her to school one day, school one day, school one
day

   C                             F  G          C
It followed her to school one day which was against the rules.

   C                             Dm             G
It made the children laugh and play,laugh and play,laugh and
Play

   C                           F      G         C
It made the children laugh and play to see a lamb at school.
```

London Bridge 4/4 Time

C
London Bridge is falling down
G C
Falling down falling down
C
London Bridge is falling down
G C
My fair lady

C
Build it up with wood and clay
G C
Wood and clay wood and clay
C
Build it up with wood and clay
G C
My fair lady

C
Wood and clay will wash away
G C
Wash away wash away
C
Wood and clay will wash away
G C
My fair lady

<u>**Are You Sleeping 4/4 Time**</u>

```
G        G        G        G
Are you sleeping, are you sleeping,
G     D     G     D
Brother John, brother John?
G                     G
Morning bells are ringing,
G              G
Everybody's singing,
G     D   G   G   D   G
Ding dong ding, ding dong ding.
```

<u>**Hot Cross Buns 4/4 Time**</u>

```
G   D    G
Hot cross buns!
G   D    G
Hot cross buns!
G          D
One a penny, two a penny,
G   D    G
Hot cross buns!


G               D
If you have no daughters,
D                 G
give them to your sons.
```

```
G               D
One a penny, two a penny,
G    D    G
Hot cross buns!

G    D    G
Hot cross buns!
G    D    G
Hot cross buns!
G               D
One a penny, two a penny,
G    D    G
Hot cross buns!
```

America The Beautiful 4/4 Time

```
 G              D
O beautiful for spacious skies,
     D7             G
for amber waves of grain
      G           D
For purple mountain majesties,
A        A7       D    D7
above the fruited plain!
G        D
America! America!
   D7                G
God shed his grace on thee
   C                   G
And crown thy good with brotherhood,
    C       D7       G
from sea to shining sea!
```

```
 G              D
O beautiful for patriot dream
     D7              G
That sees beyond the years
      G           D
Thine alabaster cities gleam
  A          A7     D    D7
Undimmed by human tears!
 G        D
America! America!
   D7                 G
God shed his grace on thee
    C                 G
Till nobler men keep once again
   C       D7  G
Thy whiter jubilee!
```

<u>Star Spangled Banner ¾ Time</u>

```
C                                    Am          D7   G
Oh say can you see by the dawn's early    light
              C        G              F       G   C
What so proudly we hailed at the twilight's last gleaming
  C
Whose broad stripes and bright stars
              Am      D7      G
through the peri - lous fight
                C       G           F      G    C
O'er the ramparts we watched were so gallantly streaming
          C                           G         G7
And the rockets' red glare, the bombs bursting in air
          C             G             Am          D7      G
Gave proof through the night that our flag was still there
        C           F           Dm          F      G
Oh say, does that star-spangled banner yet wa  -  ave
          C                     F    G      C
O'er the land of the free and the home of the brave
```

Twinkle Twinkle Little Star 4/4 Time

```
C           C       F       C
Twinkle, twinkle little star.
F     C       G7      C
How I wonder what you are.
C   F         C         G7
Up above the world so high,
C       F       C       G7
Like a diamond in the sky.
C           C       F       C
Twinkle, twinkle little star.
F     C       G7      C
How I wonder what you are.


C         Em        F       C
When the blazing sun is gone,
F       C       G7      C
When the nothing shines upon,
C       F       C       G7
Then you show your little
light,
C       F       C       G7
Twinkle, twinkle, all the
night.
C         Em        F       C
Twinkle, twinkle little star.
F     C       G7      C
How I wonder what you are.


C         E         F       C
Then the traveler in the
dark,
```

```
F           C       G7      C
Thanks you for your tiny
spark,
C       F         C       G7
He could not see which way to
go,
C       F       C       G7
If you did not twinkle so.


C         Em        F       C
Twinkle, twinkle little star.
F     C       G7      C
How I wonder what you are.
```

Take me out to the ball game ¾ Time

A7
For it's
F   D7   C   A7
one, two, three strikes, you're out at the
D7 G7   C   G7
old ball game.

C   G7
Take me out to the ball game.
C   G7
Take me out with the crowd.
A7   Dm
Buy me some peanuts and Cracker Jack.
D   G7
I don't care if I never get back, let me
C   G7
root, root, root for the home team. If
C7   F
they don't win, it's a shame. For it's
Dm   F   C   A7
one, two, three strikes, you're out at the
F   G7   C
old ball game.

<u>**A-tisket A-tasket 4/4 Time**</u>

G
A-tisket A-tasket
G
A brown and yellow basket
 D7
I send a letter to my mommy
D   **G**
On the way I dropped it
G
I dropped it
G
I dropped it
G
Yes on the way I dropped it
 D7
A little girlie picked it up
D   **G**
And put it in her pocket
        C   **Cm**
She was truckin on down the avenue
    G   **G7**
With not a single thing to do
        C   **Cm**
She went peck peck pecking all around
G   **D**
When she spied it on the ground
G
She took it
G
She took it
G
My little yellow basket
   D7   **D**   **G**
And if she doesn't bring it back I think that I will die

When The Saints Go Marching In 4/4 Time

```
C                                C
Oh when the saints, go marching in.
              C                  G7
When the saints go marching in.
   C                  F
I want to be, in that number.
            C         G7        C
When the saints go marching in.


C                                C
And when the sun, refuse to shine.
              C                  G7
And when the sun refuse to shine.
        C                        F
I still want to be, in that number.
            C    G7        C
When the sun refuse to shine.


C                                C
Oh when the saints, go marching in.
              C                  G7
When the saints go marching in.
     C                           F
I'm gonna to sing, as loud as thunder.
              C         G7        C
Oh when the saints go marching in.


C                                C
Oh when the saints, go marching in.
              C                  G7
When the saints go marching in.
   C                  F
I want to be, in that number.
            C         G7        C
When the saints go marching in.
```

Green Sleeves ¾ Time

```
    Am      C         G     Em
Alas my love, you do me wrong,
    Am                  E
to cast me off discourteously.
    Am      C     G     Em
For I have loved you so long,
    Am           E7      Am
delighting in your company.


C                 G     Em
Greensleeves was all my joy,
Am                E
Greensleeves was my delight,
C                   G     Em
Greensleeves was my heart of gold,
    Am           E7  Am
and who but my Lady Greensleeves.


        Am        C G     Em
I have been readie at your hand,
        Am              E
to grant what ever you would crave.
    Am          C   G     Em
I have both waged life and land,
        Am       E7         Am
your love and good will for to have.
```

<u>**Greensleeves Pg.2 ¾ Time**</u>

```
       Am      C         G      Em
Thy gown was of the grassy green,
         Am                    E
thy sleeves of satin hanging by,
         Am        C      G       Em
Which made thee be our harvest queen,
  Am          E7              Am
And yet thou wouldst not love me.
   C            G      Em
Greensleeves was all my joy,
Am              E
Greensleeves was my delight,
C              G         Em
Greensleeves was my heart of gold,
      Am         E7    Am
and who but my Lady Greensleeves.


         Am      C        G      Em
Well, I will pray to God on high,
         Am                   E
That thou constancy mayst see,
        Am       C      G       Em
And that yet once before I die,
        Am       E7           Am
Thou wilt vouchsafe to love me.
  C                     G      Em
Greensleeves, now farewel adue,
Am              E
God I pray to prosper thee:
C              G          Em
For I am stil thy lover true,
Am          E7              Am
come once again and love me.
```

<u>**Amazing Grace ¾ Time**</u>

```
     F                    Bb         F
Amazing Grace, how sweet the sound,
     F         Dm          C7
that saved a wretch like me.
     F     F7         Bb        F
I once was lost, but now am found,
     Dm        C7       F  Bb/C
was blind, but now I see.


     F                    Bb         F
'Twas grace that taught my heart to fear,
       F       Dm          C7
and grace my fears relieved.
     F     F7         Bb        F
How precious did that grace appear,
   Dm        C7       F       D
the hour I first believed.


G                      C         G
Through many dangers, toils and snares
    G     Em      D7
I have already come
      G            G7        C         G
Tis' grace hath brought me safe thus far
    Em          D       G
And grace will lead me home
```

<u>**Amazing Grace pg.2 ¾ TIME**</u>

```
           G                        C         G
When we've been there ten thousand years,
             G            D7
bright shining as the sun,
      G       G7        C             G
We've no less days to sing God's praise
        Em        D        G      D/E
than when we first begun.


A                       D           A
Amazing Grace, how sweet the sound,
          A        F#m        E7
That saved a wretch like me.
      A       A7          D         A
I once was lost, but now am found,
    F#m           E7        F#m   D
Was blind, but now I see.
      Bm          E        D/A      A
Was blind, but now I see.
```

<u>**It Had to Be You 4/4 Time**</u>

```
C7          FMA7    C7    FMA7
It had to be you
              D7          D7
It had to be you
                G9                  G9                      G9
I wandered around, and I finally found The somebody who
                    G9
Could make me be true
            E-7    A7      Dm7
And could make me be blue
            G7                  G7
And even be glad  Just to be sad
                C7
Thinking of you
C7                  FMA7    C7    FMA7
Some others I've seen
                D7              D7
Might never be mean
                G9              G9
Might never be cross, or try to be boss
                G9
But they wouldn't do


            BbMA7           Bbm7
For nobody else gave me a thrill
                A7      Dbdim       Dm7
With all your faults, I love   you still
            G6
It had to be you
            C7
Wonderful you
                FMA7
It had to be you
```

```
            BbMA7              Bbm7
For nobody else gave me a thrill
                  A7        Dbdim        Dm7
With all your faults, I love you still
                  G6
It had to be you
                  C7
Wonderful you
                  FMA7
It had to be you
```

NOTES